CORNWALL COUNTY LIBRARY

LYLE
Let'

J/91

TRU

TRURO
Tel. 79205

12 MAY 1987

16 OCT 1987

-4 JUN

20

222010355

25p

WITHDRAWN

CORNWALL COUNTY

LIBRARY

COUNTY HALL

TRURO

PLEASE RETURN BOOKS PROMPTLY

LET'S VISIT INDONESIA

Let's visit INDONESIA

GARRY LYLE

BURKE

© Garry Lyle 1975 and 1984
First published April 1975
Second revised edition 1984
All rights reserved. No part of this publication may be produced, stored in a retrieval system, or transmitted, in any form or by any means, electronic, mechanical, photocopying, recording or otherwise, without the prior permission of Burke Publishing Company Limited.

ACKNOWLEDGEMENTS

The authors and publishers are grateful to the following organizations and individuals for permission to reproduce copyright illustrations in this book:

Dr. Peter Abrahams; Fotolink Picture Library; G. J. G. Grieve; Indonesian Embassy; Keystone Press Agency Ltd.; Portuguese National Tourist Office; Shell Petroleum Co. Ltd.; and Richard Walker.

The cover photograph of a mother and her baby in Kalimantan (Borneo) is reproduced by permission of Dr. Peter Abrahams. The patterns on the mother's hat and the baby carrier are hand-made with beads, and the coins are real coins which were used in Kalimantan when it was a Dutch colony.

CIP data
Lyle, Garry
  Let's visit Indonesia – 2nd ed.
  1. Indonesia – Social life and customs – Juvenile literature
  I. Title
  959.8'03   DS625

ISBN 0 222 01035 5

Burke Publishing Company Limited
Pegasus House, 116-120 Golden Lane, London EC1Y 0TL, England.
Burke Publishing (Canada) Limited
Registered Office: 20 Queen Street West, Suite 3000, Box 30, Toronto, Canada M5H 1V5.
Burke Publishing Company Inc.
Registered Office: 333 State Street, PO Box 1740, Bridgeport, Connecticut 06601, U.S.A.
Filmset in Baskerville by Graphiti (Hull) Ltd., Hull, England.
Printed in Singapore by Tien Wah Press (Pte.) Ltd.

Contents

	Page
Map	6 and 7
Thirteen Thousand Islands	9
The Story of the Islands	18
Living in the Islands	34
The West End	50
In the Middle	66
The East End	79
Indonesia and the World	88
Index	93

REPUBLIC of INDONESIA
South China Sea
MALAYA
SUMATRA
Medan
Palembang
KALIMANTAN (Borneo)
Pontianak
Balikpapa
Bandjarmasin
Djakarta
JAVA
MADURA
Surabaya
Jogjakarta
BALI
LOMBOK
Indian Ocean
KILOMETRES
0
200
400
600
800
0
125
250
375
500
MILES

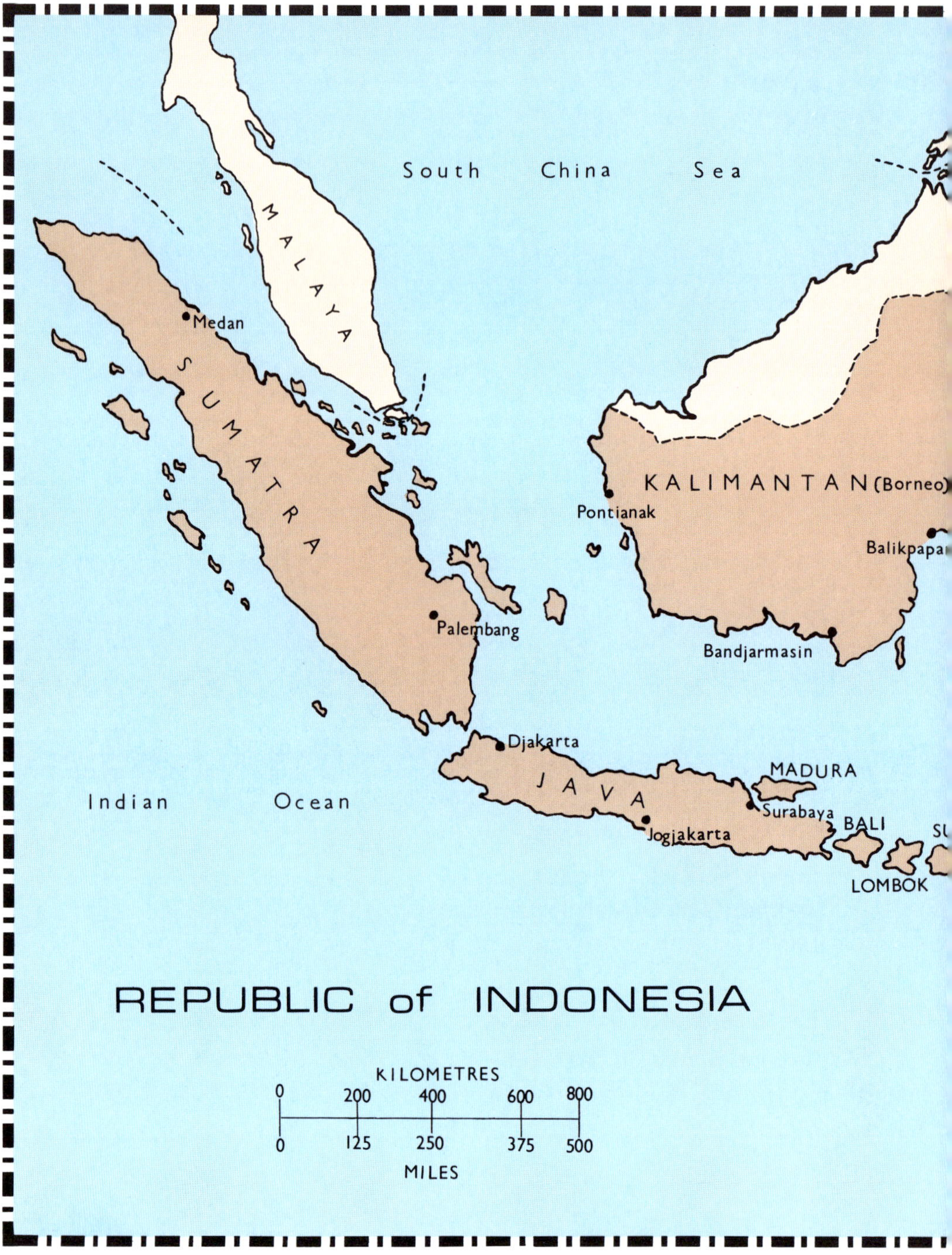

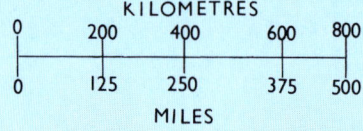

This national monument in the capital, Djakarta, is just one example of modernity in Indonesia today

Thirteen Thousand Islands

If you compare a map of the world as it is now with a map of the world as it was in 1944, you will find that over sixty countries have changed their name, or their map colour, or both. They are the countries whose people have begun to govern themselves since the end of the Second World War—countries which were once ruled by Britain, France, Holland and other European nations, but are now independent.

The Republic of Indonesia, founded in 1945, is the oldest of these new states, and one of the biggest both in size and in population. It is also one of the most difficult to govern as a single country, because its land area of over two million square kilometres (783,000 square miles) is broken up into 13,000 islands. Spreading east and west along the Equator, the 13,000 islands are part of an even bigger group that very nearly fills the 3,200-kilometre (2,000-mile) gap between Asia and Australia, where the Indian Ocean meets the Pacific Ocean.

This bigger group has three names. It is called the Malay Archipelago, because its most westerly island lies only forty kilometres (twenty-five miles) from Malaya in Asia, and because most of its people are of Malay stock and speak forms of the Malayan language. It is called Indonesia—a name made up from two Greek words meaning "Indian Islands"—because some of the first Europeans to arrive there thought they had reached India. And it is called the East Indies—short for East Indian Islands—because Europeans needed to distinguish these islands from the West Indies, which early visitors also thought to be part of India.

That explains why a world map printed in 1944 shows more than half the islands of the Malay Archipelago as a single country with the name Dutch East Indies. These islands—about 13,000 of them—had been welded into a unit by the Dutch, and governed by Dutchmen as part of Holland's colonial empire. But the island people had never been very happy under Dutch rule. So in 1945 they decided to have a government of their own, and the Dutch East Indies became the Republic of Indonesia.

Though the Republic spreads as widely as the continent of Europe or the United States of America, its main islands differ very little in appearance or in climate. Warm, wet, mountainous and very fertile, they are islands of dense tropical jungle, fast-flowing rivers, coastlines of coral sand and mangrove trees, small ricefields terraced up the slopes of peaks that are sometimes smoking volcanoes, broad plains and deep

These trees can grow up to sixteen times the height of man. Young men climb the palm trees to harvest the coconuts

valleys planted out with sugar, rubber, coffee, spices, coconut palms—in fact with everything that will grow in a climate that is often very hot but rarely very dry.

The climate is rarely very dry because sea-water evaporates quickly in the strong equatorial sun, and forms the vast cloud caps that often sit on the mountains, giving most of the islands a rainfall of between 300 and 600 centimetres (120 and 240 inches) a year. The rain comes mainly in the months from November to March, when monsoon winds from the south-west drive clouds across the whole width of the Indian

Ocean. But there is also rain in the months called the "dry season"—often more than some other countries have in their wet seasons, and always enough to keep the earth and the air damp, even with temperatures that average about 27° Centigrade (80° Fahrenheit) all the year round.

In these tropical conditions, the wildlife of Indonesia is very much what you would expect on islands that lie so close to Asia, and were probably once part of the Asian mainland. Among the wild animals are elephants, tigers, rhinoceroses, monkeys and crocodiles. There is also a huge lizard that lives only in Indonesia, and on only one island of Indonesia. It is called the Komodo dragon, and it grows up to three metres (about ten feet) long. The visitor who comes upon it suddenly may think that he has met a prehistoric monster.

The birds are noisy and colourful, and often much bigger than the birds of the cooler countries. Peacocks are common. So too are cockatoos and parrots. And in Irian Jaya (a part of New Guinea that now belongs to the Indonesian Republic) lives the "dancing" bird of paradise, with long spreading plumes of many bright colours. Wild flowers are bright and often large, too. One of them, called the rafflesia, is the biggest flower known. It grows to about one metre (three feet) wide. Unfortunately, the rafflesia smells rather like decaying meat, so you are not likely to find it decorating houses, even when the houses are big enough for it.

Of course, there are towns and cities among the Republic's vast areas of jungle and farmland. The capital city, Djakarta,

A coffee plant with its white flowers in full bloom

has a population of nearly seven million, and so is one of the world's biggest. But over 150 million people are spread throughout the islands, and of those about seven in every ten live by farming. They are mainly subsistence farmers, growing enough rice, vegetables and fruit to feed themselves, but many also produce a crop to sell, perhaps a spice like nutmeg, or kapok for stuffing mattresses and pillows. Many others do not work for themselves, but are employed on the big plantations that grow rubber, sugar, coffee, palm trees for the oil that is

A view of East Djakarta—the architecture shows the influence of the Western settlers

used in making margarine, and coconuts for the copra that is used in making soap. With spices, the products of these plantations are among the country's main exports.

Wherever the farming people work, most of them live in villages, often of only two or three long, high-roofed wooden buildings raised above the ground on poles. These buildings are called longhouses, and in them many families live together, each family having its own share of the floor space. Longhouses may be seen in towns, too, but town-dwelling Indonesian families usually prefer their own small, separate houses.

However, many town Indonesians who would like to live in separate houses cannot afford to do so. Though wages have improved since 1945, they are still very low, and Indonesian wage-earners often receive less for a whole year's work than Europeans and Americans earn in a week. Fortunately, farm-grown foods are plentiful and much cheaper than they are in Europe and America, so poorly-paid Indonesians rarely go hungry, even though they have to do without luxuries—and without many of the things that have become necessities to Europeans and Americans.

Among the town-dwelling people, there are some large

A full range of local vegetables on a typical market stall

communities of Chinese. More prosperous than many Indonesians, they are mainly shopkeepers and traders who keep to their Chinese customs and live in their own "Chinatown" areas. The population also includes some people of Indian, European and Arab descent, and as the visitor moves eastward from island to island he finds many of the people looking more and more like the dark-skinned Melanesians of New Guinea. However, the great majority of Indonesians are pale brown, and sometimes yellow-brown, in skin colour. With their straight black hair, short, slender bodies and a light, graceful way of moving, they are very much like the Malays of mainland Asia, to whom they are related. They also sound like Malays, because their main language—called Bahasa Indonesia—and most of the 250 other languages spoken in the islands are as closely related to Malayan as the speakers are related to the Malays. A visitor should not let those 251 languages worry him, by the way. If he can read this book he should have no trouble, because English is the Republic's second language. It is taught in schools, and widely used for foreign business and in the growing tourist industry.

Even though most of them are forms of Malayan, the 251 languages suggest that there may be other differences among the Indonesian people, and that is true. In fact, the Republic has chosen for its motto the Bahasa words *Bhinneka Tungal Ika*, which mean "Unity in diversity"—or, to put it another way, "We must try to act as one nation, even though many of us seem almost foreigners to each other".

An important reason for the differences is the geography of the country. With poor transport in a land of many islands, high mountains and dense, dangerous jungles, many Indonesian communities have been cut off from each other, and so have grown in their own separate ways. But the history of the country has done much towards building the differences, too. So before we look more closely at the people, we should look back over the story of their islands.

The Story of the Islands

Of the 13,000 islands that make up the Indonesian Republic, about 6,000 are now inhabited. How long all those have had people on them, nobody knows. But we do know that one of them—Java—was among man's earliest homelands. More than 500,000 years ago, when man-like creatures were first appearing, some of them lived in Java and may even have originated there. Archaeologists have found their fossilized bones, and can tell the ages of the bones from the rocks in which they were lying.

Much later—but still very early in the history of man—dark, primitive people who were men of our own kind spread slowly through Indonesia. Bones and other remains show that they spread as far as Australia and New Guinea, and it is possible that they went most of the way on foot. Many of the islands seem to have been connected at that time, not only with each other, but also with the Asian and Australian continents.

It is mainly from those very ancient settlers that the darker Indonesians of today are descended. Those of lighter skin colours—paler brown and yellowish-brown—come mostly from two waves of Malay peoples who moved into the islands between about 3,000 and 1,000 years before Christ. That was roughly the time during which the beginnings of civilization came to Britain, and the great civilization of ancient Egypt reached its height and then began to decline.

In their Asian homelands—the Malay Peninsula and parts of what is now south-west China—these Malay peoples were already on the way to civilization, and it was they who brought the beginnings of civilization to Indonesia. With the first wave came settled farming, stone tools, building in bamboo and other woods, pottery and weaving. With the second wave came metal tools and the art of working in metal, and that included the art of making metal weapons. These weapons made their

A tribal chief in battle dress, as the first Western settlers may have found him. He is carrying a metal sword

owners much more powerful than the first wave of Malay settlers, and the people of the first wave were gradually driven back into the mountains and the inland jungles. So too were the earlier, darker peoples. In time, the yellowish-brown Malays of the second wave had possession of the main Indonesian coastlands from Sumatra in the west to the Moluccas in the east, and even now a visitor finds that the rather Chinese look of many Indonesians is more noticeable on the coasts than among inland people.

With the help of some later Malay immigrants, the coastal settlers built up a civilization that was already growing old 2,000 years ago, when a new wave of migrants reached the islands. This wave, a small but very important one, came through Malaya from India. They found prosperous communities of small farmers who lived mainly by growing rice, helping each other with the difficult work of irrigating the rice and harvesting it, and giving much of their spare time to three occupations which are still widespread in Indonesia. They are gamelan music, wajang plays, and the making of batik cloth.

Batik, now a popular dress material in many countries, is made by drawing a pattern on cloth with wax, and then dying the cloth. The dye colours only those parts of the cloth which are not waxed, and so the pattern remains when the cloth is dried and the wax removed.

Wajang plays, often performed throughout the night from dark to dawn, are puppet plays. In them, the shadows of leather puppets are thrown on to a cloth screen by a bright light held between them, while a narrator called a *dalang* tells the story that they are acting—and often uses the events of the story to give the audience an object lesson in good and bad behaviour.

Gamelan music, usually heard with wajang plays as well as on many other occasions, is music played by an orchestra of stringed instruments, drums and gongs. The instruments, and

A gamelan orchestra with their decorated instruments. The sound of their music has hardly changed in two thousand years

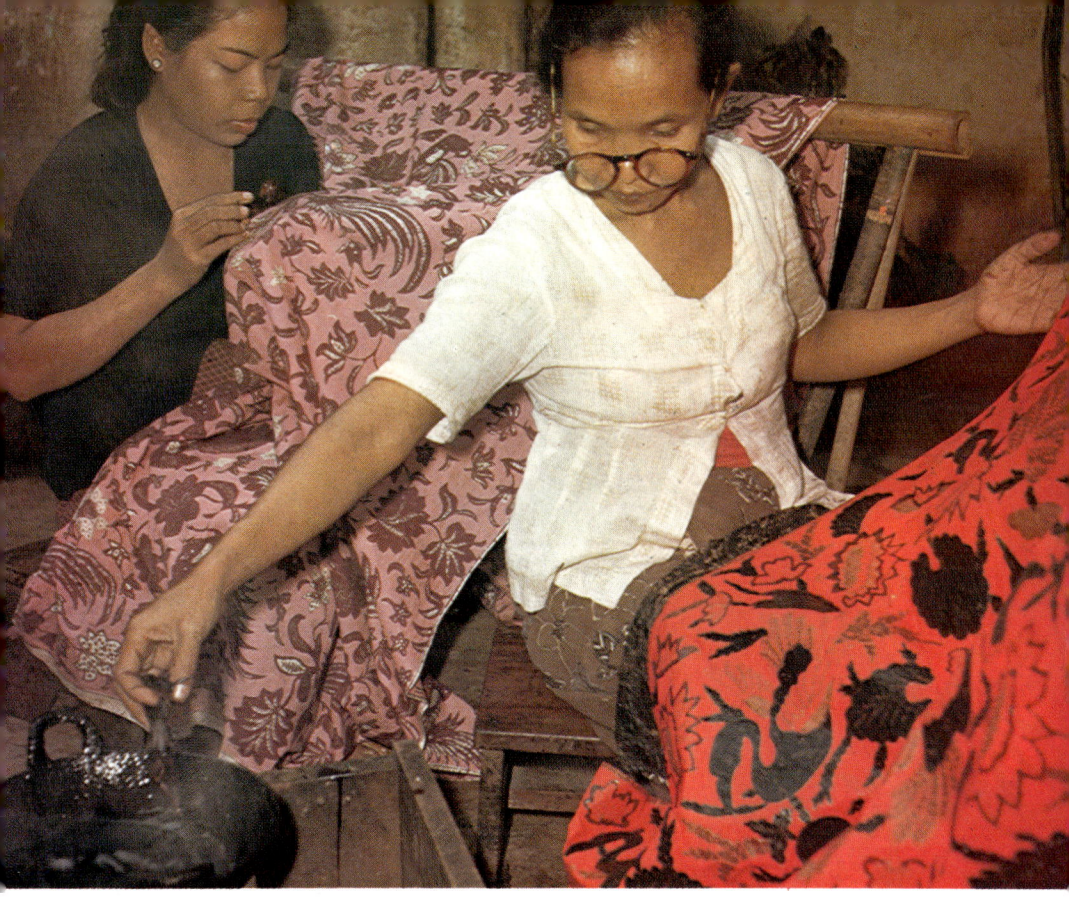
Two Indonesian women working on intricately patterned batik cloth

the high-pitched, watery music that they play, seem to have changed very little since the Indian immigrants first enjoyed hearing them two thousand years ago.

The Indians also found something that they did not enjoy. Although the Indonesians whom they met were well-advanced in civilization, their religion seemed very primitive. They believed that trees, rocks, wind, water, everything around them had spirits which could do good or evil and hear prayers.

An ancient shrine reclaimed from the jungle in Sumatra

And as some of the Indians had come as missionaries for their own more thoughtful Hindu and Buddhist religions, they were quick to try converting the island peoples. The try was very successful, though the old beliefs lived on among some Indonesians, and still live on in parts of the country.

The Indians were not content with giving Indonesia new religions. They also gave it new ways of life, and a new background to the old ways of life. Indian customs, Indian languages, Indian entertainment and Indian style of building spread widely, especially in the western half of the islands. And the small, independent Indonesian communities were gradually drawn together to make great kingdoms, under the advice and direction of Indian priests called Brahmans.

From about A.D. 600, one kingdom began to overshadow all the others. This was the kingdom of Srivijaya, on the island of Sumatra. Srivijaya became very wealthy by trading with India and other Asian countries, and remained the chief power in the island for six hundred years. Its place was then taken by Majapahit, a kingdom on the island of Java.

Majapahit did not last as long as Srivijaya, but for a time it was much more powerful. It won control over all of what is now the Republic of Indonesia, and even planted colonies on the mainland of Asia.

When the kingdom of Majapahit was just beginning, Java witnessed two events which foreshadowed the future of all the islands. The first was the arrival of some Arabs who were missionaries for the Muslim religion. The second was a visit by a European. He was Marco Polo, an Italian who had reached the islands by way of central Asia and China. Marco Polo was probably the first European to see Indonesia. He was certainly the first to be seen by most Indonesians, and so he was a great curiosity. However, apart from its curiosity value his visit did not seem very important to Indonesians at the time. They were not to feel its effects until three hundred years later.

The influence of the Indian invaders can be seen in this eighth-century Hindu temple in Java

With the Arabs, it was different. The effects of their arrival came almost at once, when many Indonesians began to accept the Muslim religion enthusiastically. This was not the beginning of the Muslim religion in Indonesia. Muslim Arab traders had been visiting the islands since about A.D. 700, soon after their religion was founded, and some of the island people had become Muslims as far back as that. But now Arab traders were growing rich and powerful, with bases that were really small kingdoms on the Asian mainland. And as trade

A sword and other relics belonging to a former Muslim ruler

links with those bases spread throughout the islands, the Muslim religion spread too. The reason for its spread was that most of the Indonesian people had never been really happy with the Hindu and the Buddhist religions. In becoming Hindus and Buddhists, they had simply followed their rulers. But the Muslim religion really did appeal to them. It appealed to them so much that their rulers thought it wise to become

Muslims too; by the year 1600, nine out of every ten Indonesians followed the Muslim faith. Buddhism died out altogether, and only the people of the beautiful volcanic island of Bali kept to Hinduism. They still do, while the great majority of other Indonesians are still Muslim.

Once again, the change of religion brought other changes. Big imperial kingdoms like Majapahit did not suit the Arab traders who had spread the Muslim faith. So when Majapahit lost its power, no other big kingdom took its place. Instead, the empire fell apart into a large number of small, separate states, each with its own Muslim ruler called the sultan. It was

A mosque (Muslim church) in Surakarta, Java

these sultans who were ruling the islands when the effects of Marco Polo's visit came at last, in the shape of European spice-traders.

Nowadays, spices are a pleasant addition to some foods, but not a very important item on grocery lists. Most of us could easily manage without them, as indeed many people do. But it was different in the time of Marco Polo, and for centuries before and after that time. Then, there was no refrigeration to keep meat fresh, so much of it had to be preserved, and the rest of it flavoured to hide unpleasant tastes when it was losing its freshness. Spices were essential, both for preserving and flavouring, and there were very few spices native to Europe. Most of them came from plants that would grow well only in countries with a wet tropical climate, countries like Indonesia. So trade with these countries was very important to Europe, and very valuable to traders. For many centuries, European traders went no further than the eastern end of the Mediterranean Sea to buy their spices. The journey from eastern Asia was left to Arabs and other Asian traders. But as tales told by Marco Polo and later travellers spread through Europe, European traders began to think that they would make greater profits by dealing direct with the spice countries—especially as the spice countries were said to be rich in gold and jewels, too.

While the only routes to the spices lay through countries closely guarded against competition with Arab traders, the Europeans could go no closer than the ports of the Mediterranean Sea. It was not until Portuguese and Spanish sailors dared to take their small sailing-ships far south in the Atlantic Ocean that traders of Europe found what they wanted—open sea-routes to the spices by way of southern Africa and America.

Spanish and Portuguese traders were quick to take advantage of the discovery. The Spaniards set up their first trading centre in Indonesia in 1521, the Portuguese a year later. British, French and Dutch traders followed them, but it was the Dutch who were most successful. By 1641 they had taken control of all the main islands except the eastern part of Timor. There, the Portuguese had a colony, but for the next three hundred years the rest of the 13,000 islands formed the Dutch East Indies, the greater and most profitable part of Holland's colonial empire.

Until 1799, the Dutch East Indies were ruled not by the government of Holland, but by a huge group of traders called the Dutch East India Company. The Company began by making enormous profits, but did nothing for the people from whom the profits were made. In fact, the Indonesians became much poorer under the Company rule. Many of the farming people became little more than slaves, forced to grow crops that the Company could export even if this left them neither the land nor the time to grow enough food for themselves. Many Indonesian traders could no longer make a living, because most trading was now done by the Company or by Chinese traders brought in to work for the Company.

Nobles relaxing in the Sultan's palace in Jogjakarta

And no one could safely resist, because the Company was allowed to keep a powerful army to see that its rules were obeyed.

However, some people did resist. They became pirates who cost the Company much of its profit by attacking Company ships and capturing their cargoes. Also, Europe was beginning to have less need for Indonesian spices. So the Company grew poor itself, and in 1790 it went bankrupt, leaving the government of Holland with 13,000 poor and resentful islands to manage.

Unfortunately for Indonesia, the government of Holland was also more concerned to make profits from the islands than to help their people. In spite of rebellions, it followed the Company in forcing Indonesian farmers to grow crops for export—not spices now, but the more profitable sugar and coffee. In addition, it stopped Indonesians from weaving cloth and working at some other manufacturing trades, so that the islands could become a market for goods made in the factories of Holland.

On the credit side, the government built railways and good

A painting showing the Indonesian leader Diponegoro leading Javanese rebels against the Dutch colonial forces in the 1820s

roads on some islands, and improved sea communications everywhere. It also gave the people better health through vaccination and other work against the tropical diseases that had always caused a very high death rate throughout the islands. However, it did little or nothing towards providing other social services, and when at last it decided to allow the Indonesians a slightly larger share in the wealth of their country the move came too late.

Throughout the nineteenth century, thoughts of independence were stirring in many Indonesians. This led to several rebellions, which the Dutch were able to quell. However, these rebellions took place only on single islands, or parts of islands. It was not until the early twentieth century that the idea of one self-governing Indonesian nation began. By the 1930s this idea had developed into a strong and united independence movement, led by the man who was to become the first president of the Indonesian Republic. He had only one name, Sukarno. Then came the Second World War, when the islands were occupied by the Japanese, and the Dutch driven out.

With the end of the war in 1945, the Japanese were driven out, too, and this gave the Indonesians their chance. Before the Dutch could take charge again, they declared their independence, and proclaimed the Republic of Indonesia on 17 August 1945. The Dutch would not accept the proclamation at first. They resisted strongly, and with military action, but the Republic survived as one of the world's new nations.

It did not survive without troubles. Like many peoples who unite in a struggle for independence, the Indonesians became disunited after independence was won. This led to a rebellion in 1965, mainly by people who thought that the new government had not been doing enough to raise the living standards that had been lowered so much by the Dutch, and made worse by the Japanese. They also wanted an alliance with Communist China, and this turned the great majority of their countrymen against them. So the rebellion failed, and was put down with a great deal of bloodshed.

Since 1965, there have been no serious political troubles, and there have been improvements in living standards for many of the people. However, there is still much to be done if all Indonesians are to benefit from the rich natural resources which—if used well—would make them the most prosperous of all new nations. Meanwhile, shall we take a quick look at the way they live now?

Living in the Islands

The 6,000 inhabited islands of the Indonesian Republic are not easy to govern as one country. Many are more than 1,600 kilometres (1,000 miles) by sea from the centre of government at Djakarta, with transport and communications which are improving but still poor. Each has its own special needs that are often in conflict with the special needs of other islands. On most, the people have their own particular customs, interests, way of living and ways of working, and these are sometimes in conflict with the plans and wishes of the government. On some, the people have their own languages, and are not always interested in trying to speak the national language. And, although nine out of every ten Indonesians are still Muslims, the common religion is not enough to ensure that all members will be content under a common national government.

Growing rice—a traditional crop in Indonesia

For the national government it is also a problem that even within each island there are usually many separate communities—often as many communities as there are villages. The people of these communities are closely tied by family links and by sharing such tasks as irrigating ricefields and harvesting crops, and they like to manage their own affairs without interference. Until the Dutch took charge, that was the

35

traditional way of life for most Indonesians. When it began to break up because the Dutch were forcing farmers to grow crops for export, many Indonesians became resentful, and their resentment helped to cause the rebellions of the nineteenth century.

Wisely, the government of the Republic has not tried to break up this traditional way of life. Instead, it encourages village communities to manage their own affairs, and provides them with money to build roads and schools, improve irrigation, clear the jungle and keep their villages free of disease.

This has made many local communities much happier with the idea of a national government, but the government still has much to do before it can feel that the nation is really united. That is why the Republic has for much of its life been what is called a "guided" democracy—a democracy in which the elected parliament has less power and responsibility than the parliaments of some older democracies. Instead, the President and his chief ministers may make plans and decisions for the whole country without consulting Parliament, and they also guide Parliament in making its own decisions.

The Indonesian President is elected, but not directly, by the people. The people elect 800 members of a body called the People's Consultative Congress, and the Congress elects the President for a term of five years. In 1983, the Congress elected for a fourth term General Soeharto, who became acting President after the rebellion of 1965, and was first elected President in 1968.

Although the members of Parliament are also members of the People's Consultative Congress, Parliament and Congress are different bodies. Congress meets only to elect a President and in times of emergency, but the 460 members of Parliament meet regularly, mainly to consider and approve of laws and plans which have been drawn up by the President and his chief ministers. An interesting and unusual thing about the Indonesian Parliament is that many of its members do not belong to political parties. Instead, they come from farmers' associations, trade unions, and groups that represent local interests of many kinds. This too helps the many separate communities of the islands to feel that they have had a real voice in the national government.

The most urgent problems facing both the government and the people of the Republic are food and living-space—but the living-space problem is not one of finding room to live. There is plenty of that. For instance, in the Republic's part of the huge island of Borneo (Kalimantan) there are only about twelve people to each square kilometre (0.4 square miles). Many other islands and parts of islands are also very thinly populated. But on Java, about half the size of Great Britain, are crowded more than ninety million people—over half of the population of the whole vast country. Add to that the population of Java's three small but equally overcrowded near neighbours: Bali, Madura and Lombok, and you have the surprising fact that seven out of every ten Indonesians are trying to live on only four of their 6,000 inhabited islands.

A road out of Djakarta. The city has its rush-hour traffic jams just like any other modern city

These four islands have become so overcrowded mainly because Java has been the centre of Indonesian trade, industry and civilization since the beginning of the Majapahit empire. Because of that, it seemed to be the island of opportunity for people who were out of work or dissatisfied with their work on other islands. But in this century there has been so much unemployment and dissatisfaction that the opportunities ended very quickly. Java itself now has a serious unemployment problem, and is also the cause of Indonesia's food problem.

As in other countries of eastern Asia, the main food throughout the Republic is rice. Sometimes eaten plain, sometimes with spiced sauces, vegetables or a little fish, it has become the main food because it is the grain most suitable for growing in warm, fertile conditions, and in Java these conditions are all at their best. Many parts of the island can produce two heavy crops in a year. However, even with double crops and every possible corner growing them, the farmers of Java cannot produce enough rice to feed over ninety million people. Nor can the other islands help. With no labour to spare (it has all gone to Java) the farmers on other islands can produce little more rice than they need to feed themselves. Indeed, in the past some of them turned to growing other crops, believing that they could always buy their rice from Java.

The result is that a country with all the right conditions for growing twice as much rice as it needs has to bring in great quantities from abroad to keep some of its people from going hungry. Naturally, the government would rather not import rice. Every bag that comes in must be paid for with money that could be used to develop parts of the islands that have never been touched by man. So in recent years many people from crowded Java have been taking part in what is called the transmigration scheme.

If a family wishes to transmigrate, the government gives it some unused farmland and a house on one of the islands that are thinly populated, sees that it is transported and settled there, and provides it with food until the land is producing its

This woman is cleaning rice kernels

own crops. In this way, many thousands of people who were unemployed and poorly fed in Java have been given the chance of a more comfortable life; and for every family that leaves Java, there is a slightly bigger share of Java's rice for those who remain. In time, transmigration could not only put an end to importing food; it could also increase the country's wealth by turning huge areas of unused land into farms growing crops for export, and by clearing from the jungles large quantities of useful timber for overseas markets that need it badly.

Of course, transmigrated families may well have to wait for schools, health services and public entertainment to reach the new settlements, but as far as schools and health services are concerned the Indonesians are used to waiting. During the three hundred years when the Dutch ruled the islands, very little was done towards educating Indonesian children. At the end of Dutch rule, the islands had no universities, only a handful of secondary schools, and so few primary schools that only seven out of every hundred Indonesians could read and write. Apart from vaccination and some other work against tropical diseases, the Dutch were also slow to look after the health of Indonesians. When they left, there was only one place in a hospital for every 1,000 people, and only one doctor for every 60,000. Most western countries have about one hospital place for every 100 people, and one doctor for every 1,000.

Since 1945, there have been very great improvements in both health services and education. Nearly all of the younger Indonesians can now read and write. Most have attended a government primary school. Many have stayed on in secondary schools. And about 200,000 are students in fifty-one universities. To match these advances in education, the government health services have very nearly wiped out a painful and disfiguring contagious disease called yaws, and are well on the way to removing some other diseases that have

The University of Indonesia in Djakarta

been common among Indonesians. They have also built up the number of hospitals to about 5,000. By western standards, some of the hospitals are equipped fairly simply, but Indonesians who are ill or injured at least have a much better chance of hospital treatment than they had before 1945. However, education and medical services have not yet reached all parts of the islands, so transmigrated families who find that they must wait for them are not alone.

Nor are they alone if they find themselves cut off by lack of transport services. There are railways on parts of Java and Sumatra, buses on those and some of the other islands, regular sea-links between many islands, and regular air-links between the main cities. The air-links are provided by the national airline, called *Garuda* after a large imaginary bird which appears in Indonesian folk stories and on the Republic's coat of arms. However, many Indonesians live long and difficult distances from the routes of Garuda and the land and sea services. If they are coastal or riverside people, they use a long canoe-like boat or small sailing-ship called a *prau* when they want to travel. If they live away from water, they usually walk. Outside the main cities, car travel is not very common even when there are motor roads, because very few Indonesian people can afford a car.

Except on the big plantations, motor-driven farm transport and equipment are also rare. Much more often, water buffaloes and oxen provide the power for farm work, but many Indonesian farmers cannot afford to have those, either. Indeed, in some places a farmer is thought to be a wealthy man if he owns even one ox or buffalo. Horses are not used for farm work, but on a few islands they are bred for riding, and the island of Sumba produces a breed of horse that is known internationally. It is named the Sandalwood, after an Indonesian tree whose pale brown, scented timber is used for making clothes-chests and other furniture.

Although he may not own a work animal, any Indonesian

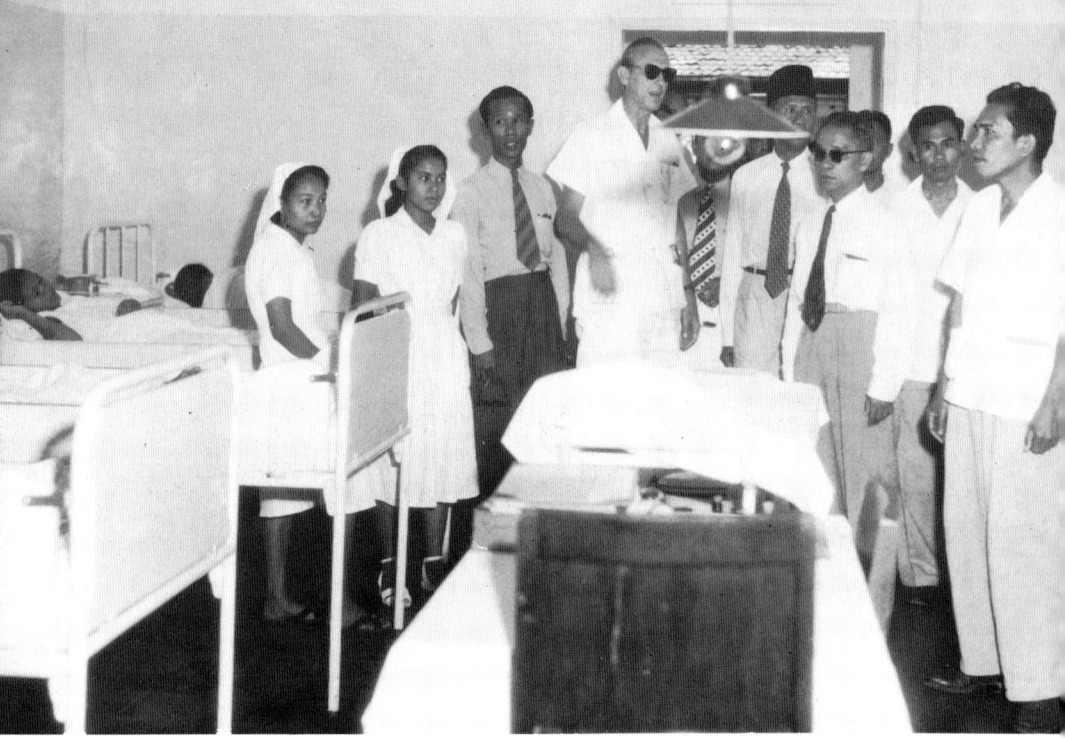

This simple hospital was built after Indonesia had gained independence. Here, visitors are being shown what progress has been made

farmer is sure to keep a large number of chickens, which often range free in and out of houses. Chickens supply the main—and often the only—meat for most Indonesians. Many farmers also keep pigs, but as most Indonesians are of the Muslim religion they are not allowed to eat pig-meat themselves. They breed the animals mainly for sale to other countries. Cattle and sheep are farmed, too, but chiefly to

Village men building a long narrow boat in the jungle

provide beef and mutton for those city people who can afford them. Very few Indonesians drink milk, and as the climate is so warm throughout the year not much wool is needed for clothing.

In the cities, most Indonesians nowadays dress in the European style, though men often top their suits with a small black peakless cap called a *pitji*. However, many city people,

A scene from the Wayang Orang ballet. Note the richly decorated costumes

and most country people, still prefer the old Indonesian way of dressing. For men, this means a jacket buttoned to the neck (or perhaps a shirt) worn over a strip of cloth wound round the waist and allowed to hang like a rather tight skirt. This is called a *sarong*. The women's skirt is longer. The usual name for it is a *kain*. With the kain, a woman wears a short jacket with long sleeves, a loose cloth headcover and sometimes a scarf—all usually in bright colours and often of the patterned cloth called *batik*.

The richly-embroidered and jewelled national costumes

often seen in films and tourist advertisements are not everyday wear. Usually very valuable and very old, these costumes are handed down from generation to generation, and are used for special occasions such as weddings, and for the dances and festivals that are the main entertainment for most Indonesians. On Bali, perhaps the most famous of all Indonesian islands, there are no less than eighty-two days of festivals and similar celebrations every year.

Apart from festivals, *wayang* and other plays by puppet or human actors, and *gamelan* or similar music, radio is the only form of public entertainment available everywhere. Each of the Republic's twenty-seven provinces has its own government broadcasting station. These bring even the most remote islands

Batik and other traditional craft goods on sale in Bali

An Indonesian man in his traditional dress

within receiving range and, as small transistor receivers can be bought very cheaply, nobody has to do without sound broadcasting. Many Indonesians also listen to the British Broadcasting Corporation's overseas programmes, broadcast from London in the Bahasa Indonesia language.

However, television has not yet spread very far. At present, less than five per cent of the Republic's total area is within range of the government's television services, and in any case the price of a television receiver is well beyond most Indonesian incomes. On the other hand, cinema seats are not at all expensive. Even the small towns usually have their cinemas, and Indonesians are very enthusiastic film-watchers.

Many are also enthusiastic about entertaining themselves with traditional arts and crafts. Visitors often come away feeling that there are more part-time weavers, painters, embroiderers, carvers and jewellery-makers in the Republic than in any other country of the world; and they are probably right. In the past, Indonesians followed these crafts partly to amuse themselves and add a little decoration to their own houses and bodies, partly to earn a little extra income by providing decoration for their neighbours' houses, or perhaps for some public building like a temple. But their main object nowadays is to provide souvenirs for the growing numbers of tourists who find Indonesia an ideal place for a tropical holiday. Fortunately for the tourists, the Indonesians are a very artistic people, with a long tradition of fine craftsmanship in beautiful styles to guide them. So—unlike the souvenirs of many other countries—a souvenir from Indonesia is something well worth having for its own merits, not just a carelessly-made and rather ugly memento of a happy tour abroad. And that brings us to our own short tour of the islands.

The West End

The twenty-seven provinces of the Indonesian Republic are fairly new divisions. Their boundaries were set simply to divide the total land area into parts small enough for easy government. So an Indonesian rarely thinks of himself as belonging to a particular province in the same way as an Englishman belongs to a county or an Australian to a state. Nor is it usual for a visitor to notice whether he is in one province or another. Instead he is much more likely to notice that the country divides itself into three large groups of islands—a western group, a central group, and an eastern group.

The western group lies closest to the Asian mainland, and so was the first to receive the Malayan settlers who were the ancestors of most modern Indonesians. It also contains the most fertile island (Java), three of the biggest single land areas (Java, Sumatra and Kalimantan) and the widest range of natural resources. So it is easy to see why the western group has always been the home of Indonesian civilization, and why it was quick to become the centre of trade, industry and government for all three groups of islands.

Remembering that Sumatra lies much closer to the Asian mainland, it is perhaps not so easy for us to see why Java was quick to become the main island of this western group. Nor is Java's very fertile soil and double rice crop the whole

A view of paddy fields, where the rice is being cultivated in terraces

answer. Parts of Sumatra are very fertile, too, and the reason for the fertility of both islands is the same—volcanoes. Wherever there are volcanoes, minerals blown out during eruptions enrich the surrounding soil, and both Java and Sumatra are very volcanic areas. Each island has a spine of high volcanic mountains rising to over 3,000 metres (10,000 feet). Some of the volcanoes are active now, and others have been active in fairly recent times. Indeed, the most violent eruption known to history took place on a small island between Java and Sumatra in 1883. This island, named Krakatoa, is a partly submerged section of the volcanic ranges that run through the bigger islands. Its volcano had never been thought very dangerous, but the eruption of 1883 blew half of the island to pieces. People nearly 5,000 kilometres (over 3,000 miles) away heard the sound of the explosion, and ash forced up through the crater spread right round the world. The eruption also caused tremendous tidal waves, which wrecked many villages on the coasts of Java, Sumatra and some smaller islands, and drowned over 36,000 people.

Luckily for Java and Sumatra, violent eruptions are rare. Their large share of Indonesia's one hundred active volcanoes are usually very gentle, and do much more good than harm, by keeping the soil fertile. However, Sumatra has a smaller amount of very good soil than Java, even though Java is only about one third of Sumatra's size. Also, much of Sumatra's good soil is less suitable for rice-growing than Java's, and has been used for growing export crops like rubber and tobacco. Java has therefore been able to feed from its own soil about five times as many people as the larger island could, and with this much higher population has been able to develop a wider variety of industries. Among the many hundreds of different products of these industries are motor-cars, bicycles, radio sets, cotton cloth, chinaware, chemicals, shoes, plywood and—on the offshore island of Madura—enough salt to meet the needs of the whole country and leave some over for export. For a time, Java was also an important oil-producing island, but that is one of the few industries in which Sumatra has drawn ahead. Nowadays, very little oil is produced in Java, while about four-fifths of the Republic's huge output comes from Sumatran fields. Even so, the headquarters of the oil industry remains in Java.

The other reason why Java has become the main island of the western group is that it lies closer to the rest of Indonesia than Sumatra does. In earlier times, this allowed Javanese merchants to capture and hold the sea-trade with islands producing spices and other goods needed by foreign traders.

An oil rig in operation in the jungle at Kawengan, East Java

Spectacular scenery in Sumatra

And so the seaports of Java became great storehouses of goods awaiting export, and the main goal of foreign shipping.

These seaports are spread along the north coast, from Tandjung Priok at the western end to Surabaya in the east, and are linked by a coastal railway built when the island was a Dutch colony. Sheltered by the small cattle-raising island of Madura, Surabaya is the Republic's biggest and most important shipping centre. It is also a seaport well-known to readers of adventure stories, and a manufacturing city with factories making cloth, chemicals and glass.

However, visitors from abroad are more likely to enter Java through the seaport of Tandjung Priok or the Djakarta international airport, because these are the gateways to the huge, overcrowded city of Djakarta, which is the capital of the Republic and was the capital of the Dutch colonies. Like the railway which links it with Surabaya, modern Tandjung Priok was built by the Dutch. They needed a new seaport for the capital because the capital's own harbour was silting up, and had become too shallow for big ships. The Dutch also built much of the capital city itself. Then called Batavia after the Roman name for the ancient people of Holland, it replaced an earlier town named Djajakarta, and the Indonesians have now brought back the old name, shortened to Djakarta.

At a first glance, Djakarta seems a prosperous and comfortable city, spreading out from a centre of luxury hotels and glassy office blocks to garden suburbs left by the Dutch. How-

A view looking north over Djakarta—a city bursting at its seams

ever, a second glance shows a very different city—a city bursting at its seams with a population that has swollen from half a million to nearly seven million in fifty years, and is now much too big for it.

In the short and often difficult thirty years of the Republic's life, its governments have had neither the time nor the money to solve this problem, and the people of Djakarta have rarely been able to help themselves. Most of them are very poor, and many are unemployed. The result is a city where the visitor has only to step behind the modern skyscraper blocks around Merdeka (Freedom) Square to find himself in vast slums of rickety bamboo-framed huts with poor drainage and sanitation, very few other conveniences, and a risk of disease that is among the highest in the modern world.

Since the country settled down after the rebellion of 1965, both the national and the city governments have been doing their best to improve these conditions. Djakarta has been made a "closed city", which means that people are no longer allowed to move there in the hope of finding work. Most of its streets have been re-surfaced and made suitable for modern traffic—a very necessary improvement, as they had been breaking up and crumbling to dust through lack of repair. Water, sometimes pumped by windmills, has been laid on to some of the huge "shanty-town" areas. Electricity has reached some of them, too, and the authorities have been trying to make them less crowded by moving some of the people to more comfortable houses on the outer edges of the city.

However, Djakarta must also use builders, building materials and money for the factories, the shops and the tourist attractions that will help to solve its unemployment problem. So progress with its housing and health problems has to be very slow—and even as a "closed city" its population is growing by about 200,000 every year. Perhaps a better and quicker solution would be for half of Djakarta's people to remember that Indonesians are not city-dwellers by nature, and to spread themselves over the many islands where there is room to live comfortably in the traditional way.

Much less crowded than Djakarta, and much more pleasant to look at even on a second glance, is the old city of Jogjakarta, Jogja for short. On the south coast, Jogja is a university town, a town of craftsmen in silver, and a town of ancient buildings that go back to Majapahit and even earlier kingdoms. It is also a volcano town. Close behind it rises the high volcanic peak Mount Merapi, active though so far not dangerous. The smoking crater of Mount Merapi is an impressive sight, but Jogjakarta has a man-made sight that is even more impressive. It is an enormous shrine of the Buddhist religion, climbing in nine terraces round the sides of a hill. Called Borobudur, it was built 1,200 years ago in honour of Buddha, and the five kilometres (three miles) of terraces are walled with stone-carvings of scenes from Buddha's life.

Huge as it is, Borobudur was lost for nearly one thousand years. Probably because a violently erupting volcano drove them away, the people who built it and looked after it disap-

A contrast to modern Djakarta: some of the primitive and overcrowded houses on the outskirts of the city

peared in about A.D. 900. Nobody took their place for a long time and, by then, the shrine had been covered by jungle growing in layers of volcanic ash. It was not until 1814 that the top terraces were uncovered, and only in our own century has the whole shrine been seen again. However, it is still not seen as the Javanese of one thousand years ago saw it. Much of the stonework has been broken or worn away by weather, and several friendly nations have been helping the Indonesians to restore it.

Also in the Jogjakarta area are the famous Hindu temples of Prambanan, built during the years of the Majapahit empire. The Prambanan temples are famous not only as great works of stonemasonry and sculpture, but also because they are used as a floodlit background for a very beautiful and popular Indonesian dance entertainment called the Ramayana Ballet.

The old market Jogjakarta

Though none are as big as Java's, Sumatra too has its cities and its city problems. When the Dutch left, only the rubber and oil centre of Palembang had enough people to make it a city, but now the island has seven cities. The largest of these is Medan, with its seaport Belawan facing Malaya across the Strait of Malacca, and the nearest Indonesian city to the Asian mainland. Only a village at the beginning of this century, Medan is now a centre of the rubber industry, of university education, and of the Muslim religion. Its mosque (Muslim church), though not remarkable to look at, is the biggest in the Republic.

South of Medan, also on the Strait of Malacca, another town has been growing quickly. This is the seaport of Dumai, where tankers are loaded with crude oil from the very rich oil-fields of central Sumatra. Some of these fields are in remote jungle areas without roads, so workmen and equipment have to be flown in by helicopter. The oil comes to Dumai by pipeline—a pipeline so wide that aircraft passengers can see it snaking through the jungle. Because Sumatran oil is very thick, it must be warm before it will flow through the pipes. This makes the pipes warm—and so, on chilly nights, the jungle people leave home to come and sleep on them.

Sumatra's other oil centre, Palembang, has also become much bigger with the expansion of the island's oil industry. However, the growth of cities and populations need not worry Sumatra so much as it worries Java. Unlike Java, Sumatra is overcrowded only in parts, and is not fully developed. Indeed,

This jungle area has been developed to provide facilities for transporting crude oil from Sumatra (where it is drilled) to Java

Among
are man
who wo
little of t
the min
nesian p
Dyaks a
primitive
mainly i
on or nea
bamboo
who live

This long
headman

some of Java's surplus population has recently moved to the southern part of Sumatra under the government's transmigration scheme, and is growing rice on land reclaimed from the jungle.

The jungles themselves can also provide employment. They contain vast quantities of timber suitable for building and for furniture-making, and the timber industries are still very small compared with the amount of raw material to be had from the vast tree-covered mountainsides.

The mining industry too is still much smaller than it could

61

Fishing boats on the shore. The village house has been built on stilts in the water

place, but float them up the rivers on trading trips among the riverside Dyaks.

Some of these Malays are descended from people who came direct to Borneo from the Asian mainland. The rest are descendants of Indonesians who "transmigrated" from other islands during the period of Dutch rule and earlier. One large group of these, a Muslim people called the Malanau, crossed from the neighbouring island known to the Dutch as Celebes. Nowadays, Celebes has gone back to its Indonesian name Sulawesi, and when we have crossed from Borneo to Sulawesi we are in the Republic's central group of islands.

In the Middle

Sulawesi is about 190,000 square kilometres (73,000 square miles) in area, yet every part of the island is well within 112 kilometres (seventy miles) of the sea. You will understand why if you find Sulawesi on the map, and think about its rather odd shape—a shape which has been likened to a somewhat squashed octopus, and explained as "a handful of peninsulas tied in the middle".

Because of its shape, Sulawesi has a much longer coastline and more sheltered water than most other islands of the same size, and for this reason the Sulawesi people have always been famous as sailors and shipbuilders. One group of them, from Makasar in the south-west, were also famous as pirates until late in the nineteenth century. They preyed on shipping in and near the Makasar Strait between Sulawesi and Borneo, and did much towards making the old Dutch East India Company an unprofitable business.

Though Muslim in religion and partly of Malay stock, the Makasarese are also related to a more primitive, pagan people who live in highly decorated boat-shaped houses in some of the remoter parts of southern Sulawesi. Called the Toradja, they look—and sometimes behave—rather more like Pacific Islanders than Malays, and another look at the map will tell you why. Sulawesi is very near the halfway mark between Asia and Australia, and so is just as likely to have been in touch with the Pacific Islands as with south-east Asia.

Sulawesi is also the home of two other peoples who differ from most of their fellow-Indonesians. These are the Toala, and the Minahassen. The Toala—a short, dark, flat-nosed people—are very primitive indeed. Like similar people on two small islands near Sumatra, they are probably the last of a very ancient Indonesian community related to the Australian aborigines. In the past, some of the Toala were used as slaves by other Sulawesi peoples, and their descendants now live in the more settled parts of the island. The rest live a quiet, primitive life in the jungles, and get their food mainly by hunting animals and gathering wild crops.

The Minahassen are very different in behaviour and, surprisingly, slightly east European in appearance. Many of them are tall, with pale skins and even pinkish cheeks. Nobody knows exactly where they came from, but they were certainly well established on Sulawesi when the first European traders (Portuguese) arrived there in 1512. Hostile and violent in the early days of European settlement, they were later converted to Christianity, and are now one of the few Christian communities in the Indonesian Republic. Perhaps because they may have some European ancestry, they took very easily to European ideas, education and habits, and were on friendly

Women sorting tobacco leaves and tacking them together before drying

terms with the Dutch colonial government. They usually spoke Dutch in preference to their own language, and many worked in government offices and as teachers in government schools. Even more became policemen, and soldiers in the Dutch army, and many of these supported the Dutch against the Indonesians who wanted independence.

In their home territory—the northern arm of Sulawesi—the Minahassen produce what is now the island's main export: copra. The other cultivated parts of the island also produce copra for export, as well as rice, maize and tobacco. With the help of water pumped up the hillsides by hydroelectricity, much of the rice is grown in small, wet, terraced paddy-fields, as it is on the hillsides of Java. However—in spite of what many people believe—it is not necessary to have flooded fields to grow rice. Provided there is good rainfall at the right time, it may also be grown in "dry" fields, like wheat and other grain crops. And, in fact, it is grown in "dry" fields in many parts of Indonesia, including the coastal plains of Sulawesi.

Sulawesi also exports some of the resins used to make varnish, and sulphur gathered from solfataras—holes in the ground which become encrusted with sulphur brought up by volcanic vapour. But it no longer exports the ingredients of a product which made the name Makasar famous. That is Makasar (or Macassar) oil, which men of the Victorian era used to rub into their hair and which caused their wives to cover the backs of armchairs with washable strips of cloth called anti-macassars.

South-west of Sulawesi, and immediately south of the Makasar Strait, lies a small and very mountainous island named Lombok. Overcrowded with people who could not find room on Java, Lombok has over 270 people to the square kilometre (0.4 square miles) against Kalimantan's twelve, and is not a pleasant place to live in as conditions are now. Indeed, many of its 1,300,000 people find it difficult to live at all, as Lombok is one of the few parts of Indonesia where people can really go hungry. Because of unusually dry "wet seasons", it has had two serious famines in fairly recent years, one of them so serious that it caused about 20,000 deaths. However, it is only over-crowding that has made the trouble. With a population to match its size, Lombok would be as comfortable as any other Indonesian island.

Apart from its distressingly over-large population, a visitor's main memory of Lombok is an imaginary line. Called the Wallace Line, it runs south from the Makasar Strait past the western coast of Lombok, and that makes Lombok the most westerly part of what was once the Australian continent. Many thousands of years ago—but perhaps after the Australian aborigines had arrived on the present continent—all the Indonesian islands from Lombok eastward were joined to Australia, and all the islands to the west of the Wallace Line were joined to Asia. Geographers know that because they have traced the old edges of both continents far below the sea, but for visitors who are not interested in underwater surveying there is enough clear evidence on the surface of Lombok. If they look at the vegetation, they will see types of palm and other trees that are common in northern Australia but found nowhere west of the Wallace Line. If they look at the birds, they will see the mound-builders and cockatoos of Australia, but hardly any of the birds that are common not only on the Asian mainland, but even on the island of Bali, just a short sea distance west of Lombok. And these Australian characteristics grow more and more noticeable as the Indonesian islands spread eastward to Timor and then across the Arafura Sea to New Guinea.

A view of the vegetation found on Timor, which is east of the Wallace Line. It is similar to the vegetation found in New Guinea and Australia

With Sulawesi and Bali, the islands spreading eastwards from Lombok to Timor make up the central group. Though Timor is no longer partly Portuguese, the island is still divided into two parts. However, the native people of both parts are less civilized, and less Malayan in appearance, than the people of the western islands. With dark skin and frizzy hair, they look more like the Papuans of New Guinea, to whom they are related. Most of them live in high-roofed, one-roomed, wooden

Native village people of Timor standing outside their thatched houses which are raised on stilts

houses, raised above the ground on stilts and thatched with palm-leaves. Their main occupation is producing their own food—chiefly maize, rice and pig-meat—and breeding the native ponies, which they ride very well. They also help in producing rubber and copra, and in taking sandalwood from the forests—all for export.

The islands between Timor and Lombok can be counted in

hundreds, but only three are bigger than Lombok, and most are very much smaller. The three bigger islands are Sumbawa, Sumba and Flores, all well known for their sandalwood. Indeed, Sumba—where the Sandalwood horses are bred— was once known to Europeans as Sandalwood Island. Sumbawa also breeds horses, and on all three islands large numbers of cattle are raised. The main reason why these islands in particular raise cattle and horses is that they have a lower

A house of traditional design in western Indonesia. It was built to house several families

A Hindu temple on Bali. Bali is the only island of Indonesia whose population remain Hindu in religion

annual rainfall and more natural grassland than most of Indonesia.

Like the Timorese, most of the people have a rather Papuan appearance, and though many of them are now Muslim or Christian in religion they are often fairly primitive in their way of life and are still attached to pagan customs such as animal sacrifice. This is especially so on Sumba, which has less Muslims and Christians than Sumbawa and Flores, and where horses are regarded as holy animals by many of the people.

Muslims and Christians are also in a minority on Bali, the only central island west of the Wallace Line, but here the reason is that nearly all the people follow the Hindu religion. This is a survival from the centuries when neighbouring Java

A Rangda, or witch mask which is used in festivals in Bali

was the centre of the great Hindu empire Majapahit. Majapahit lost the last of its power in 1478, when its army was beaten by one of the new Muslim kingdoms. The last king refused to surrender to the Muslims, and killed himself, but his son and a large number of Indonesian Hindus escaped to little Bali (then very sparsely inhabited) which was only a short sea journey from the eastern end of Java. There, they set up a new Hindu kingdom which remained separate from Muslim Indonesia until it became part of the Dutch East Indies and then the Indonesian Republic.

In its way of life, Bali is still separate. Its most interesting buildings are Hindu temples. The most enjoyable of its many entertainments are festivals of dancing, music and stage-plays

A popular tourist attraction—the traditional Balinese Legong dance. This dance has great religious significance and each hand movement has a different meaning

connected with the Hindu religion. The themes of its art and craft work (and the Balinese are fine artists and craftsmen) nearly all come from Hindu ideas and stories. In fact, Bali is in many ways a living "museum" of all civilized Indonesia as it must have been before Arab traders and European colonists brought new ways of living and thinking.

That is one reason why large numbers of tourists prefer Bali to other islands of the Republic, and why many foreign artists and students settle there for long periods. Another reason is that Bali is the most beautiful of the Indonesian islands. Everything is good to look at, from the sacred volcano Gunung Ajung, 3,050 metres (10,000 feet) high and very dangerous, to the white coral sand. And the island's only problem is that there are too many people for the food that its very fertile soil can produce. Ruggedly mountainous and dangerously volcanic, it does not allow many people to live at the higher levels,

The sacred volcano Mount Gunung Ajung, Bali

and so most of a population of nearly two and half million crowd the lower land at about 700 to the square kilometre (0.4 square miles)—an even higher rate than in Java. To increase the problem, some of the land is taken up by farmers who produce palm oil, coffee, cattle and pigs for export. The result is that Bali, like Lombok, sometimes suffers from famine.

Unfortunately, the Balinese like Bali. To many Muslim Indonesians, one island is very much like another. If they move from Java to, say, Sumatra or the coastlands of Kalimantan they will find a way of life very much like their own. But if a Balinese leaves Bali there is no place in the Republic that can offer him living space against an ancient Hindu background like the one he has left behind him. So the transmigration figures from Bali are very low. The great majority of Balinese prefer to stay at home and run the risk of hunger.

Otherwise, they might do well to consider a move to the eastern end of the Republic.

The East End

European traders—and indeed the much earlier Arabs—first came to Indonesia in search of spices. They found them on most of the inhabited islands, but above all in a north-eastern section that came to be known as the Spice Islands.

Also called the Moluccas by Europeans, and Maluku by Indonesians, the Spice Islands spread over the sea area between Sulawesi and New Guinea, and into the Pacific Ocean. Most of them are mountainous and volcanic, with thick jungle in which such spices as cloves, pepper and nutmeg still grow wild. But among the high islands are scattered some which lie much lower—often just above sea-level. Unlike the high islands, these are not the remains of a broken-up land mass. They are coral islands, formed by the action of the sea on coral reefs, and some of them are still being made.

Because they often lack water, and sometimes soil too, many of the coral islands are uninhabited; and those that are inhabited rarely produce more than food for their people. It was the richer high islands that attracted Europeans to this part of Indonesia—especially the southern half of them, which are grouped round an island called Ceram.

Ceram is by far the biggest of the southern Moluccas, and because it has oil-wells it is also the most important to modern

Indonesia. However, in earlier times it was much less important than a very small island named Ambon, or Amboina. Only 1,010 square kilometres (386 square miles) in area, Ambon lies off the south-west corner of Ceram, with open sea to the south, and so was in a very good position for the early foreign traders. By sailing there, they did not have to risk being trapped by enemies among the maze of islands further north. And because the rulers of Ambon were friendly to the Dutch and to the Portuguese before them, Ambon became a great warehouse for the spices of all the Moluccas. It also became the centre of Dutch colonial government in the Moluccas, and is now the centre of the Molucca, or Maluku, province of the Indonesian Republic.

As a result, Ambon has nearly as many people as Ceram, although Ceram is about seventeen times its size. Even so, it is far less crowded than some of the westerly islands, while Ceram has only about six people to the square kilometre (0.4 square miles). The rest of the Moluccas—north and south—are also thinly populated. The biggest island in the north, which on a map looks oddly like a small version of Sulawesi, has only three people to the square kilometre. The island, called Halmahera, was an important Japanese base during the Second World War, and the scene of many battles between Japanese aircraft and bombers from the Australian and American bases in nearby New Guinea.

As the Moluccas lie so close to New Guinea, their original people were close to the dark, frizzy-haired New Guinea

A cassowary, the largest species of bird to be found on the island

jungled mountain ranges rising as high as 5,030 metres (16,500 feet). Within the mountains lived one of the world's most primitive peoples, tribesmen still at the level of the Stone Age. Until the Second World War, many of them had never seen a European, or even an Asian, and outsiders who tried moving among them often did so at the risk of their lives.

Even now, an outsider cannot be sure of his safety in some mountain areas. He could meet with tattooed, cannibal spearmen wearing bones through their noses and feathered head-dresses—spearmen who have possibly watched aircraft flying over their jungled valleys, but never laid eyes on the kind of people who travel in them. And there were many more of those at the end of the Second World War, especially in the western half of New Guinea. In that part of New Guinea, tens of thousands of tribespeople did not know that their country had been invaded and captured by the Japanese, and then recaptured by Americans and Australians.

On the coastlands, the New Guinea people were rather more civilized. Some had been educated by Christian missionaries. Many had worked on plantations managed by Europeans, or for the Australian and United States armies which were based in New Guinea for war service. But they were still mainly tribespeople. They did not think of themselves as a New Guinea nation, much less as members of an Indonesian nation. Indeed, few of them even realized that New Guinea was an island of the Indonesian Archipelago, and only a small

A tribesman from the mountainous area of Irian Jaya, in full tribal dress

number of them had any of the Malay blood that is shared by the great majority of the modern Indonesian people.

However, in 1945 the western half of New Guinea was governed by the Dutch, and the newly-independent Republic of Indonesia felt that it was entitled to take over all of Holland's Indonesian possessions. Until 1962, Holland disagreed, and held its New Guinea colony, but in that year the United Nations Organization decided that the Republic should be given the chance to govern it. Holland accepted the decision, and from 1963 the Republic's land area was increased by 416,000 square kilometres (161,000 square miles) and its population by 758,000 people.

Neither the land nor the people had been given much attention by the Dutch. The people had always lived by very primitive farming. They dug in small fields with sharpened sticks cut from the jungle with stone axes. They grew tropical root vegetables like yams, and fast-growing fruits like paw-paws and bananas, and they moved to newly-cleared fields after every two or three harvests because they did not know how to keep the soil fertile. Most of them were still farming in that way when western New Guinea became part of Indonesia. Nor had the Dutch gone very far with developing the country for themselves. After more than one hundred years, only about 100 square kilometres (forty square miles) had been put to growing crops—mainly coconuts—for export.

It was the same with education and health. The Dutch trained a few young men from the tribes as government officers, and allowed missionaries to have schools in some places, but left the rest of the people as they were. As for health, it was not until the armies moved in during the Second World War that there was any serious attempt to control malaria and the other tropical diseases that had made Dutch New Guinea a very unhealthy country for its native people as well as for foreign settlers.

For the Dutch, the difficulty was that they found western New Guinea too big, too undeveloped and too expensive to manage. They had quite enough to do and to pay for in their other Indonesian colonies. So western New Guinea had to be left until improvements could pay for themselves. And—in spite of oil discoveries—that time was still not in sight when the Republic of Indonesia took over.

Now called Irian Jaya or Irian Barat, western New Guinea

Husking coconuts. The dried flesh—copra—is the main export of this area

has not so far given the Republic any important advantages apart from the oil-wells. Nor can it hope to gain many more advantages until a great deal of money and skill are given to educating the people, improving their farming methods, and opening up what is still largely a wild and half-known country. The Republic has done as much of that as its other problems have allowed, especially in education. There are now government schools in even the very remote areas, and the country has its own university in the small seaport town that is its capital. People who try to find this town on atlas maps are sometimes confused because different maps give it different names—the Dutch name Hollandia, the New Guinea name Kotabaru, and the Indonesian names Djajapura and Sukarnapura. However, Djajapura is now the official name.

In developing Irian Jaya, the Republic has been receiving help from other countries, and also from some New Guinea people who have been quick to see that development could improve their living standards. However, most of the people are not so interested, and they are often unco-operative. There have ever been rebellions against the new government. So progress is very slow. Irian Jaya is still the most backward part of the Republic, still in every way far behind the eastern half of New Guinea, which is now called Papua-New Guinea. The Papua-New Guinea people—after some guidance from the Republic's neighbour Australia—are now governing themselves as an independent nation.

Indonesia and the World

The new Republic of Indonesia had bigger aims than adding western New Guinea to its territory. It also imagined the Malayans of south-east Asia and the neighbouring Philippine Islanders as part of a great community of Malay peoples, with the Republic as its leader, and tried to interfere with the plans and politics of both.

Neither the Malayans nor the Philippine Islanders liked this interference, and a serious quarrel arose when Indonesian guerrilla fighters began helping rebels in the Federation of Malaysia (also newly-independent), while Malaysians crossed to Sumatra and helped rebels against the Republic.

By then, the government of the Republic was on friendly terms with Communist China, which was also helping the rebels in Malaysia. On the other hand, the Indonesians had reason to believe that Britain and the U.S.A. would use Malaysia as a base to force a change of government on the Republic. In fact, Britain and the U.S.A. were already sending supplies to the rebels in Sumatra. And all those things very nearly caused war between the Republic of Indonesia and the Federation of Malaysia.

However, in 1965 the Republic made its own change of government, and the new government set out to co-operate with its neighbours rather than to interfere with them and to try forcing itself upon them as their leader. It joined Malaysia, the Philippine Islands, Thailand and Singapore in forming the Association of South-East Asian States, and it stopped supporting the policies of Communist China, which were as unpopular with most Indonesians as they were with the other peoples of the Association.

Since then, the government of the Republic has been concerned with making some very necessary improvements at home rather than with expanding abroad. Apart from transmigration, these include the launching of many new industries which can make wider and better use of the country's rich natural resources; and an attempt to bring modern methods and modern equipment to old industries—particularly farming and fishing.

Engineers assembling a Bailey bridge for an oil pipeline

Foreign investment provides opportunities to expand Indonesia's natural resources. This is a view of a modern oil complex with a large tanker waiting to ship the crude oil to the western world

The seas around the Indonesian islands contain more fish than any other waters in the world, but until recently these had hardly been touched except by inshore fishermen working from canoes and small sailing-boats with hand nets and lines. Nor had the Indonesians gone very far with fish "farming" in the fresh water used for irrigating ricefields, as is done in some other rice-growing countries. However, with the new methods and equipment that are coming into use, both sea water and

Wide roads through the jungle leading to the site of a new bridge. Modern communications enable farmers and industrialists to market their produce more easily

fresh water could give the Indonesians not only as much fish as they need for themselves, but also large quantities for export.

Harvests of rice and other crops are also growing bigger as farmers learn to make better use of their land, as new roads and better transportation make it easier for them to market their produce, and as factories are provided for treating such crops as cassava and peanuts. The peanuts are crushed for their oil, and starch is taken from the huge cassava roots to make tapioca, which for many Indonesians is an alternative food to rice.

To improve her farms and her fisheries, as well as to expand her timber, mining and factory industries, Indonesia has asked for—and received—much help from the United Nations Organization, and from three countries with whom she was not very friendly before 1965. They are the U.S.A., Japan and Australia. Australia has provided money, equipment and staff training for over thirty Indonesian industrial projects, and both Japan and the U.S.A. are supporting many more.

At the same time, the Republic has been playing a useful and much-respected part in the work of the United Nations Organization, where Indonesians are seen as a people who fit very closely this character sketch by one of their own ambassadors: "Indonesians accept and welcome discussion of problems. And they seek compromise. We continually strive for harmony in life, and try to avoid conflict. This does not mean that we will not fight for our fundamental beliefs. But for us, conflict is a profoundly regrettable last resort, and one to be shunned."

Index

Africa 29
Amboina, Ambon 80, 81
America, Americans 15, 29
animals, farm 43–45, 54, 72–74, 78
animals, wild 12, 67, 70, 82
Arabs 16, 24, 25, 27, 28, 76, 79
Arafura Sea 70
area 9, 66, 80
arts 19, 49, 76
Asia, Asians 10, 12, 16, 18, 19, 24, 25, 28, 39, 50, 60, 64, 67, 70, 83
Atlantic Ocean 29
Australia 18, 67, 70, 82, 84, 87, 92

Bali 27, 37, 47, 48, 70, 71, 74–78
Balikpapan 62
Bandjarmasin 62
Batavia 55
batik 20, 46
Belawan 60
birds 12, 70, 82
Borneo 37, 62, 64–66
Borobudur 57
Brahmans 24
Britain, British 9, 19, 29, 88
broadcasting 47, 48

cajeput oil 82
cassava 91, 92
Celebes (*see* Sulawesi)
Ceram 79, 80
China, Chinese 16, 18, 20, 24, 29, 33, 63, 82, 88, 89
cinema 48
climate 11, 12, 28, 39, 69, 74
cloth 20, 31, 46
clothing 45–47
coconuts 11, 14, 82, 85
coffee 11, 13, 31, 78
copra 14, 62, 68, 72, 82
crafts 19, 49, 57, 59, 76

dancing 47, 59, 75
Djajapura 87
Djakarta 12, 34, 55–57, 62
Dumai 60
Dutch 10, 29, 32–36, 41, 54, 55, 60, 63, 65, 68, 75, 80, 81, 85, 86
Dutch East India Company 29–31, 66
Dyaks 63, 64

East Indies 10
education 16, 36, 41, 42, 57, 68, 86, 87
Egypt 19
Equator 9
Europe, Europeans 10, 15, 16, 24, 28, 29, 30, 67, 76, 79, 83, 84
exports 14, 29, 31, 36, 54, 68, 72, 85

factories 57, 91, 92
festivals 47, 75
fish, fishing 62, 81, 89, 90, 91, 92
Flores 73, 74
flowers 12
food 15, 37–40, 67, 69, 72, 77–79, 82, 85
France, French 9, 29
fruit 13, 85

government 32, 34–37, 50, 56, 68, 85, 89
Gunung Ajung, Mt. 77

Halmahera 80
health 32, 36, 41, 42, 56, 57, 85, 86
Holland 9, 29–30, 55, 81, 85
Hollandia 87
hospitals (*see* health)
houses 12, 14, 15, 49, 56, 57, 62, 63, 66, 72, 82

imports 39
India, Indians 10, 22–24

93